MAKE ME LAUGH!

PUNNY PLACES

JOKES TO MAKE YOU MAPPY

by June Swanson
pictures by Brian Gable

Carolrhoda Books, Inc. • Minneapolis

Q: What's the wettest mountain in the world?

A: Mount Rainier.

Q: How does a rancher comb her hair?

A: With a sagebrush.

Q: What kind of ears do the Smoky Mountains have?

A: Mountaineers.

Q: What kind of ears do the Alps have?

A: Glaciers.

Q: Why are the mountains like ocean waves?

A: They both have whitecaps.

Q: What did the sheriff say after he climbed the mountain?

A: "I need arrest."

Q: Do you think those mountain goats know where Mount McKinley is?

A: I don't know. Alaska and go find out.

Q: What did the roadrunner think about the Grand Canyon?

A: It was just gorges.

Q: Where's the desert cemetery?

A: In Death Valley.

Q: Why couldn't the mountain keep a secret?

A: Its brooks babbled everything.

Q: What do you have when surfers raise their hands?

A: Swaying palms.

Q: What kind of music sounds like a mountain landslide?

A: Rock and roll.

Q: What did the cactus do to get everyone out of its way?

A: It blew its thorns.

Q: What would you call a yellow stripe painted down a mountainside?

A: A mountain lion.

Q: What is the border between two oceans called?

A: A sea lion.

Q: What do you get if you cross the Mojave Desert with a grandfather clock?

A: The sands of time.

Q: Which streets lead to a roundup?

A: Roadeos.

Q: Who was Dorothy looking for in the desert?

A: The Lizard of Oz.

Q: Why did everyone laugh at the mountain?

A: Because it was hill-arious.

Q: How do you decorate a cactus for Christmas?

A: With thornaments.

Q: Why did the archeologist leave the desert?

A: Her job was in ruins.

Q: What's the difference between a hill and a pill?

A: A hill is hard to get up, and a pill is hard to get down.

Q: Where do outlaws live?

A: In the Bad-lands.

Q: Why are leaves in a high wind like outlaws?

A: They are rustlers.

Q: Why did the whale rush to scratch his back on the reef?

A: Because he knew an itch in time saves nine.

Q: When is a mountain like a car out of gas?

A: When it's MT.

Q: How did the sun heat the ocean?

A: One ray at a time.

Q: How did the magician describe a mirage?

A: "Now you see it, now you don't!"

Q: What do you find in both a hill and a mountain?

A: The letter "i."

Q: What did the coyote say when she heard the jackrabbit was leaving the desert?

A: "Oh, well, hare today, gone tomorrow."

Q: What instrument did the little Alp want to play?

A: A Matter-horn.

Q: What part of a rancher dries out the fastest?

A: His legs. They're always chapped.

Q: What did the farmer raise in the sand?

A: A beach umbrella.

Q: What did the codfish drive to the beach?

A: Her Codillac.

Q: What did the bear use when he played baseball on the mountain?

A: His sum-mitt.

Q: What would you have if Mount Rushmore threw a football to Pike's Peak?

A: A mountain pass.

Q: How did one clam call the other clam?

A: On his shell-ular phone.

Q: Why won't the lobster ever run out of money?

A: He lives in a bank full of sand dollars.

Q: What did one mountain say to the other mountain after the earthquake?

A: "It wasn't my fault!"

Q: How did the little camel describe her trip across the desert?

A: "Easier said than dune."

Q: How did the police drive to the beach?

A: In a squid car.

Q: What did the cactus say to the bank teller?

A: "I needle little money."

Q: Why did the ballerina go to a flat place on the mountain?

A: To do a pla-teau dance.

Q: What spice grows on a ranch?

A: Sage-brush.

Q: What does a desert doctor always carry?

A: A thirst aid kit.

Q: How did the doctor take the little cactus's temperature?

A: With a thornometer.

Q: Why couldn't the waves reach the shore?

A: They were tide up.

Q: Why wouldn't the skeleton climb the mountain?

A: He didn't have the guts to do it.

Q: Where do you save your water in the desert?

A: In the Thirst National Bank.

Q: How could you tell the artist was tired of drawing mountains?

A: She went back to the drawing bored.

Q: What do you call a beach party?

A: A shell-ebration.

Q: What lives in the Rockies and is red and black and white all over?

A: A ladybug in a snowstorm.

Q: What's round, lives in the desert, and bites people?

A: A mesquite-o.

Q: What's the little rattlesnake's favorite song?

A: "Snake, Rattle, and Roll."

Q: How did the Big Bad Wolf know the Little Pig was building a strong house in the mountains?

A: He saw Himalayan the bricks.

Q: What did the hiker say when she stepped on the cactus?

A: "Yucca!"

Q: What do you have when the desert sun shines down a jackrabbit hole?

A: Hot, cross bunnies.

Q: What do you get if you cross Pike's Peak with an alarm clock?

A: Mountain time.

Q: What do you get if you cross Pike's Peak with a pair of sandals?

A: Cold feet.

Q: What do you call fudge made in the desert?

A: Sandy candy.

Q: Why couldn't the whale hear the ocean roar?

A: Because she was hard of herring.

Q: What has 14,162 feet and no legs?
A: Mount Shasta.

Q: Who puts baby camels to bed?
A: The sandman.

Q: Who plays for the beach parades?

A: The bass band.

Q: When is a mountain goat most likely to go into a log cabin?

A: When the door is open.

Q: In what month was the little Alp born?

A: Alp-ril.

Q: Where does King Crab live?

A: In a sand castle.

Q: What do you have when 400 wild blueberries try to get down the mountain at the same time?

A: A blueberry jam.

Q: What has four wheels, two horns, and goes from rock to rock down the mountainside?

A: A bighorn sheep on a skateboard.

Q: Why did the kitten meow all day?

A: She was practicing her Cat-skills.

Q: Who crosses the mountain going trip-trap-giggle, trip-trap-giggle, trip-trap-giggle?

A: Three silly goats gruff.

Q: What did Dorothy say as she climbed the mountain?

A: "Lions and goats and bears, oh my!"

Q: Who cleans King Crab's sand castle?

A: The mermaids.

Q: Where does the wise old desert owl live?

A: In the sagebrush.

Q: Which law officers live in swamps?

A: Marsh-alls.

Q: How can you tell when a cactus has a magnetic personality?

A: Its needles point north.

Q: Why did the cactus call the dune a sissy?

A: The dune wouldn't stand up to him.

Q: Why did the mountain goats and the bighorn sheep meet on the mountaintop?

A: They knew two herds are better than one.

Q: What do you call wranglers who are always hungry?

A: Chowpokes.

Q: What did the little Alp eat at noon?

A: Her avalunch.

Q: Who is green and never comes down the mountain?

A: Hermit the Frog.

Q: In what month was the little sandstorm born?

A: Au-gust.

Q: Why did the baby snake cry?

A: She lost her rattle.

Q: Why wasn't the shark sorry when he bit the large fish?

A: He did it on porpoise.

Q: Why was the little mountain pine always warm?

A: Because she was a fir tree.

Q: What goes "clap-clap-ouch, clap-clap-ouch?"

A: A cactus playing pat-a-cake.

Q: Why was the father hill worried about the baby hill?

A: He was afraid the baby would never a-mountain much.

Q: Why is everyone on the Gobi Desert friendly?

A: Because there are no-mads there.

Q: Where do seahorses live?

A: In barn-acles.

Q: What expert ranchers are good at fishing?

A: Wr-anglers.

Q: What did the artist use to draw a mirage?

A: Disappearing ink.

Q: What do you call a dog who lives on a mountaintop?

A: A chilly dog.

Q: What did the cactus call its trip to the barbershop?

A: A needleless experience.

Q: Where do sea turtles live?

A: In shell-ters.

Q: What lives in the mountains of China and is black and white and red all over?

A: A sunburned panda.

Q: Did you hear the news about the blowing sand?

A: It's all over the desert.

Q: What kind of bear lives in the ocean?

A: A bear-acuda.

Q: Why did the bare mountaintop blush?

A: She thought the other mountains were peaking at her.

Q: What did the glacier's bumper sticker say?

A: "Have an ice day!"

Q: Why couldn't the shell move?

A: She was conched out.

Q: Why did the bear look for a scale on the mountain?

A: Because where there's a hill, there's a weigh.

Q: What street can be found in every horse corral?

A: Mane Street.

Q: How do you get to the ocean?

A: Go left at the tern on the beach.

Q: Where did the fisherman cook his Rocky Mountain trout?

A: On the mountain range.

Q: What did the desert cardplayer say when he picked up his hand?

A: "O-asis!"

Q: How can you tell when the ocean's friendly?

A: The tidal wave.

Q: How did the ocean announcer end her program?

A: "Tuna tomorrow for the next exciting chapter."

Q: Was the rancher hurt while sleeping in the pasture with his cattle?

A: No, the experience just grazed him.

Q: Why is a seagull on the beach like the North Pole?

A: They both have sandy claws.

Q: Why did Rudolph go to the desert?

A: He was looking for the Santa Fe Trail.

Q: What happened after the camper waited for the sun to rise over the mountain?

A: It finally dawned on him.

Q: What did the little mirage do for the desert talent show?

A: A disappearing act.

Q: What falls on the mountain and never gets hurt?

A: Snow.

Q: Why did the gambler go to the desert?

A: He was looking for a hot tip.

Q: Where is Smokey Bear's hat?

A: On top of old Smokey.

Q: How often did Jonah go to the beach?

A: Just once in a whale.

Q: What did one volcano say to the other volcano?

A: "Do you lava me?"

Q: What did Cinderella lose at the beach?

A: A glass flipper.

Q: Why didn't the shark bite Donald?

A: Donald ducked.

Q: Why was the mountain climber sad?

A: She was wearing her blue jeans.

Q: What did the astronaut start when she climbed the mountain?

A: An avalaunch.

Q: What would a farmer have if a cactus grew in his hayfield?

A: Needles in a haystack.

Q: Why did the crab go to the beach?

A: To see the ocean wave.

Q: What did the Swiss hiker yell as he fell down the mountain?

A: "Alp! Alp!"

Q: What do you call it when camels run from one waterhole to the next?

A: Oases races.

Q: What new hobby did the cactus take up?

A: Needlepoint.

Q: What do you call the ocean's comings and goings?

A: Current events.

Q: What did the cowpoke say when he tried to saddle the moving horse?

A: "Doesn't this Mount Everest?"

Q: How did the nomads hide on the desert?

A: They used camel-flage.

Q: What's the weather like on Mount Everest?

A: I don't know. I've never been able to climb it.

Q: Did you hear the story about the bare cactus?

A: It was pointless.

Q: What happened when the coyote left his fishing worms in the desert sun?

A: He heated debate.

Q: What patriotic song is a rancher's favorite?

A: "The Star-Wrangled Banner."

Q: Why was the sun waiting for spring to come to the mountain?

A: It wanted to burn over a new leaf.

Q: What instruments do ranchers play?

A: Saddle horns.

This book is available in two editions:
Library binding by Carolrhoda Books, Inc., a division of Lerner Publishing Group
Soft cover by First Avenue Editions, an imprint of Lerner Publishing Group
241 First Avenue North
Minneapolis, MN 55401

Website address: www.lernerbooks.com

Library of Congress Cataloging-in-Publication Data

Swanson, June.
    Punny places : jokes that make you mappy / by June Swanson ;
pictures by Brian Gable.
        p.   cm. — (Make me laugh)
    Summary: A collection of jokes about different places.
    ISBN: 1–57505–647–X (lib. bdg. : alk. paper)
    ISBN: 1–57505–703–4 (pbk. : alk. paper)
    1. Riddles, Juvenile. 2. Puns and punning—Juvenile literature
[1. Jokes. 2. Riddles. 3. Puns and punning.] I. Gable, Brian, 1949– ill. II. Title.
III. Series.
PN6371.5 S865 2004
398.6—dc21   2002151102

Manufactured in the United States of America
1 2 3 4 5 6 – JR – 09 08 07 06 05 04